SOME NOTABLE
18th CENTURY
STAFFORDSHIRE M.Ps.

John Godwin

SOME NOTABLE 18th CENTURY STAFFORDSHIRE M.Ps.

by

John Godwin

STAFFORDSHIRE COUNTY LIBRARY

© 1984 by John Godwin
and Staffordshire County Council

My most grateful thanks to Herman Dyson, Divisional Librarian of Staffordshire County Library, for his unfailing help and courtesy in obtaining books and documents needed for the preparation of this booklet, and for offering help and advice in so many ways. With his continued assistance, it is hoped in due course to produce a companion booklet; Some Notable Nineteenth Century Staffordshire M.Ps.

Design advice and art work by Ivan Taylor of Staffordshire County Education Department's Audio Visual Section

Typed by Vivienne Simpson and printed by Staffordshire County Council's Central Print Unit

ISBN 0 903363 25 9

Staffordshire County Library Headquarters
Friars Terrace
Stafford

CONTENTS

Chapel of St. John the Baptist, Cotton

Buildings on the south side of New Palace Yard

LIST OF ILLUSTRATIONS AND SOURCES

The illustration shown below and the decorations reproduced on various pages
are specimens of sculpture that were in St. Stephen's Chapel. All come from
J.T.Smith's Antiquities of Westminster, 1807. This Chapel was made over to
the Commons for their meeting place by King Edward VI in 1547. It was destroyed
by fire in 1834.

FOREWORD

I suppose we all have our own ideas about the qualities an ideal M.P. should possess. This booklet gives brief glimpses of some Staffordshire M.Ps. of the past, and it is left to readers to make their own judgments as to the suitability of these gentlemen for the positions they occupied. It will, I am sure, be agreed by all that their qualifications were extremely varied! I have chosen some for what they did in Parliament; others for what they did not do in Parliament; and a few because they performed notable achievements outside Parliament. However, whilst all were elected for a constituency in Staffordshire within the 18th century, some continued into the 19th century.

In the period of history to which this book relates, relatively few people were entitled to vote, and before the 1832 Reform Act there were many glaring anomalies in election procedures. Little or no account had been taken of movements in population over the past years when delineating constituencies; thus many towns (for example, Stoke-on-Trent) were unrepresented in Parliament. In a few cases, places in England with no, or practically no, population at all - the people having long since left - were still represented in Parliament. Notable examples were Old Sarum in Wiltshire, which was an uninhabited mound of earth, and Dunwich, most of which had for many years been submerged under the North Sea following continuous erosion of the coastline. No wonder the House of Commons was described in 1820 as 'unconstitutional...glaringly absurd and ridiculous...founded on no rational principle of either population, intelligence or property'.

The position regarding representation in Staffordshire was that before the 1832 Act there had been ten M.Ps. (two for the County; two for Tamworth; two for Lichfield; two for Stafford and two for Newcastle-under-Lyme). Under the provisions of this Act the County representation was increased to four (two for the north and two for the south); Stoke-on-Trent was allotted two; Wolverhampton two; and Walsall one. Other towns were represented as before. This made seventeen M.Ps. in all; an increase of seven.

Elections in England for the County members seem to have followed a fairly consistent pattern. Every holder of freehold land worth forty shillings or more had the vote. The usual election procedure was for the Sheriff to call a meeting of voters. Nominations for Parliament were made at these meetings, and those nominated - who, of course, had to be property holders themselves - either accepted or withdrew. Where only the required number of the nominated persons accepted, the election was concluded there and then. If more persons than the number allotted as M.Ps. to the County accepted nomination, the meeting was called upon to choose the required number by show of hands. But this did not usually satisfy the unsuccessful candidate, who demanded that the Sheriff conduct a poll of those eligible to vote.

Polling booths were set up on the appointed day and those who came to vote were required to declare their qualifications. Then they publicly declared their vote for a particular candidate. Voting often continued for several days. Many unauthorised voters attempted to circumvent the qualifications, and in order to check on this the names of the individuals were later checked against the Land Tax Returns. Often, objections to the procedure were registered by the agent of the candidate who could, as a last resort, petition the House of Commons if he felt there had been irregularities. Elections were colourful affairs, and often gangs of thugs stood around as an inducement to voters to declare their vote for a particular candidate.

Elections in the boroughs of England before 1832 were organised in a similar way by the Mayor, but here there was no uniformity of entitlement to vote. Some boroughs had a relatively wide franchise; in others voting was restricted to a few holders of special positions. Some gave the vote only to members of the Corporation or to those who had the freedom of the borough; and there was another category which gave the vote to householders who had a separate fireplace in which to cook their food!

As far as the pre-1832 position was concerned in the Staffordshire boroughs, Lichfield gave the vote to any forty shilling freeholder and also to any resident freemen who paid the local taxes. Burgage holders - those who were tenants of land held by the lord for a yearly rental - could also vote. At Newcastle-under-Lyme, all resident freemen could vote. This freedom could be obtained by sons of existing freemen, by those who were apprenticed to a freeman, or through special powers granted to the Corporation. In Stafford, freemen had the vote, while at Tamworth all residents who paid 'scot and lot' (local taxes) were entitled to vote.

But it was the important families in the area who often exercised the greatest influence over electoral events. For example, the Leveson-Gowers, who had lived at Trentham since 1668, had exercised political influence since 1675. From the mid-eighteenth century, every contested seat in Staffordshire County, or in Lichfield or in Newcastle-under-Lyme, and even sometimes in Stafford, was an attempt to reduce the political influence of this family.

The Gowers were originally Tory in their affiliations, but in the 1740's Lord Gower married a daughter of the Duke of Bedford, and joined the Bedford Whigs, thus upsetting County politics. In the mid-eighteenth century the family took a particular interest in Lichfield politics - in which city they had considerable property - and here they shared control with the Ansons. Thomas Anson (1695-1773), the elder brother of the famous sailor Admiral George Anson, was the founder of the Whig party in Staffordshire, and the Tory leader at the same time was Sir William Bagot. Subsequent members of the Anson family, who had been living at Shugborough since 1625, carried on the strong Whig tradition.

The Ansons and Gowers were influential and clever enough to prevent any election contests at Lichfield for nearly forty years. This was done by creating faggot votes - votes manufactured for party purposes by the transfer to persons not otherwise qualified of sufficient property in Lichfield to qualify them as electors. They kept control over the faggot voters by providing mortgage facilities on the advance required to pay for the property. The property owners could live anywhere in England, and in fact many resided in Trentham, Shugborough, Lilleshall, and other places.

It is hardly surprising that many Lichfield electors, realising this jiggery-pokery of the Ansons and Gowers, reacted with surliness and even with hostility towards their Members of Parliament. The city was dominated by Whig politics for many years, in spite of all the hostility, and for a long time no-one sat for the city without the express approval of the Ansons and the Leveson Gowers. This situation continued until well after the Reform Act of 1832, though after 1825 the Gower influence in Lichfield was reduced because much of the Lichfield property of the Gowers was sold to Lord Anson.

In Stafford and Newcastle-under-Lyme the creation of faggot votes was impossible, as the franchise was much more closely defined. So other tactics were employed, and outright bribery was one of these. The expense of elections, and the dividing line between legitimate expenses and bribery, was a source of long-standing grievances. It must be remembered, however, that some of the methods that would be considered legitimate one hundred and fifty years ago - for example, providing free drinks for one's supporters at the local public houses - would be considered as malpractices today. Money was often left by candidates or their agents at local public houses, so that the electors could drink whenever they chose until the money was gone. Free food for the burgesses was often provided. Many of the burgesses in Newcastle-under-Lyme lived in cottages owned by the Leveson Gowers, and they paid no rent. This was another way of making sure of votes, as the tenants had the knowledge that, if they did not vote as they were expected to do, they could be charged for arrears!

In addition, votes were often openly purchased. The usual going-rate for a 'plumper' - a vote for one candidate only, instead of for the two allowed - was at least ₤5. Stafford had become notorious for bribery and corruption at election times for a number of years.

We may wonder why the Leveson Gowers should wish to play such a prominent part in the politics of Newcastle-under-Lyme, and indeed of the County, for so many years. Their money and their social position were maintained by marriage into the right families and by taking advantage of political situations, so it may be assumed that they considered the return of their candidate to Parliament to be very necessary to maintain their status. It was in the last quarter of the eighteenth century that opposition to this family began to become widespread, in spite of their lavish gifts to the Corporation at Newcastle-under-Lyme. But it is worth bearing in mind that much of the opposition came not from those guided purely by altruistic motives, but rather from groups who were led by considerations of their own self-interest. Even when, early in the nineteenth century, the Leveson Gowers began to relinquish their overt political grip on events in Newcastle-under-Lyme, their influence behind the scenes with the Corporation did not relax. But the tactics of the Corporation in creating more and more freemen to counteract any political threat became self-defeating in the end because it became increasingly costly to buy votes at subsequent elections. The ordinary voter was quite unconcerned as to the person elected to Parliament, unless some vital issue of direct concern - for example, Catholic emancipation - was at stake. Most voters would gladly give their vote to those who made it most worth their while, in spite of threats from the other side.

It says much for the influence of the Leveson Gower family, however, that they were able to nominate both seats at Newcastle-under-Lyme for almost a hundred years, from the year 1747 onwards, and that they were able to influence politics in the County at large for so long.

In Tamworth, only the Thynnes of Drayton Manor had been able to nominate candidates successfully; though other families had tried to do so. By 1765 the Townshend family of Tamworth Castle had agreed with the Thynnes that each family should nominate one candidate, and after 1790, when Robert Peel senior bought the Thynne's property for ₤132,000, the arrangement with the Townshends continued. It worked up to a point, though local opinion was not a force that could be completely ignored and, for example, in 1820 Robert Peel, senior, withdrew his nomination rather than face an independent candidate who was strongly favoured.

✕✕✕✕✕✕✕✕✕

1.   'OROONOKO CHETWYND' or 'BLACK WILL'

WILLIAM RICHARD CHETWYND was Member of Parliament for Stafford 1715-1722; Plymouth 1722-7; and Stafford 1734-1770.

He was the 3rd son of John Chetwynd of Ingestre Hall, Stafford, and his wife Lucy, daughter of Robert Roan of Chaldon, Surrey, was born in 1684 at Rudge, Standon, Staffordshire.

He was educated at Westminster School and matriculated at Christ Church, Oxford on 8th June 1703. In 1707 he entered the Middle Temple, but shortly afterwards in 1708 he was made Envoy to Genoa, an appointment which he held until 1712.

On 28th January 1715 he entered Parliament as an unopposed representative for Stafford, the other representative being his brother Walter, who was created 1st Viscount Chetwynd in the peerage of Ireland in 1717. In mid-1715 William married Honora, daughter of William Baker, formerly British consul at Algiers. It is thought that she brought with her a considerable fortune. There were two sons and four daughters of the marriage, but she died 1st September 1726.

On 16th April 1717 Chetwynd having been appointed a Lord Commissioner of the Admiralty, an office of profit, a new writ was issued for a by-election in Stafford, but William was re-elected unopposed on 25th April 1717 and he held the seat until the next general election in 1722, when both he and his brother lost at Stafford after a very riotous contest. However, William was returned for Plymouth, and continued his appointment at the Admiralty until 1727 when he resigned. He did not stand for election at Stafford in 1727 but his brother Walter was elected. However, Walter was appointed Governor of the Barbadoes and on 1st May 1731 a new writ was issued at Stafford. Although William had intended to stand he did not do so as there was 'interest against him'.

In the election of 1734, fought very bitterly 'under the disturbing influence of Stafford ale', William Richard Chetwynd was returned and held the seat at Stafford for the rest of his life. There was a by-election on 31st January 1738 and William's brother John, 2nd Viscount Chetwynd and Recorder of Stafford 1735-67, was elected unopposed. He served Stafford alongside William until the 1747 election.

The Earl of Wilmington became Prime Minister in 1741 and it was to his good offices that William Chetwynd owed the appointment of Master of the Mint, a post which he held from 29th December 1744 to 3rd June 1769. It was a very lucrative job. In 1745 he was Under-Secretary of State, which he held for three years.

The following year, 1746, it is said that the Duke of Cumberland stayed with William at Chetwynd House, Greengate Street, Stafford whilst Cumberland's army camped at Stone, daily expecting an encounter with the Pretender's forces. Some mystery surrounds the actual date when Chetwynd House was built. In The Chetwynds of Ingestre mention is made that 'the next election contest at Stafford (1747) was accompanied with more riots, and though Chetwynd was again successful, no less than eighteen persons were indicted at the Assizes in 1748, "for breaking into and defacing" his new house'. The Court awarded him satisfaction for the injury to his house, but he 'graciously declined to accept it'. The use of the words <u>his new house</u> certainly implies that it had been built recently but, whilst acknowledging this the <u>Victoria County History</u> Volume VI suggests it was built c.1700, whilst Pevsner says 'the house looks Queen Anne' (1702-14). It is possible, that William had it built for his wife on their marriage in 1715 and it may have been known as his 'new' house for many years.

Chetwynd House, Stafford

By 1754 William Richard Chetwynd's active political career was over and he had become a regular supporter of the government. There had been some enmity between the Walpoles and the Chetwynds for some years and this culminated in March 1743 when William and 'old' Horace Walpole (1678-1757) came out of the House of Commons arm-in-arm, then proceeded to fight a duel actually within the precincts of the House. William Chetwynd was slightly injured. Twenty years later, however, when Chetwynd was living in Dover Street, London, Horace Walpole (1717-97) related how: 'Will Chetwynd ... verging on four score, still rode his journeys from Stafford to London, while younger men travelled by Flying Coach or in their own carriage-and-six.' In 1764 he writes: 'Old Will Chetwynd, now past eighty, and who had walked to the House, did not stir a single moment out of his place from three in the afternoon till the division at seven in the morning.'

On 21st June 1767 he succeeded his brother John as the 3rd Viscount. The Viscountcy, being of the Irish peerage, did not confer a seat in the House of Lords so Chetwynd continued to hold his seat in the Commons. On 18th March 1768 this remarkable man, William Chetwynd, who was known as 'Oroonoko Chetwynd' or 'Black Will' because of his exceeding swarthiness, was returned again for Stafford, but died on 3rd April 1770 aged 86. He was buried in the Church at Ashley and his executors paid the usual penalty of ₺5 'for burying in linen'. A monument to his memory was placed in Ashley Church, but is no longer there. Commissioned by William's daughter, Deborah, who held an appointment at Queen Charlotte's court and was instrumental in obtaining for Josiah Wedgwood his first royal orders, the monument was designed by James Stuart (1713-1788). Wedgwood, who had been on a friendly footing with the 3rd Viscount, contributed a basalt vase to the design.

William Richard Chetwynd, apart from building one of the finest houses in Stafford, took a great interest in the town. He was Mayor in 1742, 1750 and 1763.

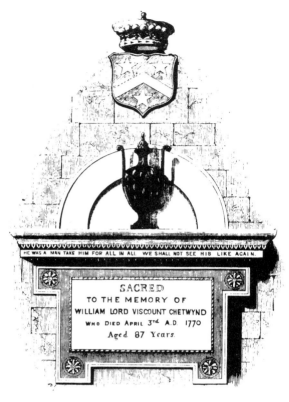

Monument to Lord Chetwynd

---

2.   'OLD DICK'

RICHARD VERNON was Member of Parliament for Tavistock 1754-61; Bedford 1761-74; Oakhampton 1774-84; and Newcastle 1784-90. He was born on 1st June 1726 and was the fifth son of Henry Vernon (M.P. for Stafford 1711-15) of Hilton Park, between Cannock and Wolverhampton. Hilton Park gave its name to the Hilton Park Service Station on the M6.

After touring Italy and France, Richard was commissioned in November 1744 with the rank of Ensign in the 1st Foot Guards, and became Lieutenant then Captain in 1747. In October 1751 Vernon resigned his commission. At that time he had become closely connected with the Duke of Bedford who thought highly of him. Even Horace Walpole described him the following year as 'a very inoffensive young fellow, who lives in the strongest intimacy with all fashionable young men'. In 1757 he became second secretary to the Duke of Bedford, then Lord Lieutenant of Ireland.

On 15th February 1759 he married Lady Evelyn, daughter of the 1st Earl Gower (1694-1754), widow of the 1st Earl of Upper Ossery and sister of the Duchess of Bedford. Evelyn died in 1763 and there was a daughter of the marriage, Henrietta, who married the 2nd Earl of Warwick in 1776.

A few months after his marriage Vernon was given an Irish sinecure, Clerk of Quit Rents, but in 1761 he received a pension in lieu of that office. When Bedford joined the Grenville Administration in September 1763 Vernon received the office of Clerk Comptroller of Green Cloth which he retained, on and off, till 1782. After the death of the Duke of Bedford in 1767, Vernon followed the Leveson-Gowers in politics.

He did not get office again but perhaps by then he did not need the money, for his parliamentary career is of minor significance when compared with his career on the Turf. His wagers are recorded as early as 1751, where he is mentioned as 'Captain Richard Vernon, alias Fox, alias Jubilee Dicky', and he achieved a great reputation as one who placed his bets and wagers very skilfully. At Newmarket, he entered into a partnership (as far as horse racing was concerned) with the 4th Duke of Queensbury (known as 'Old Q'). So successful was Vernon that it was said that he 'converted a slender patrimony of £3,000 into a fortune of £100,000' before quitting the Turf.

He owned and bred a large number of horses, and was one of the original members of the Jockey Club. In 1768, when the Jockey Club Cup was competed for, 'Old Dick' as Vernon was often called, won the trophy; and nine years later, with Glory, an Arabian horse, he won the Ascot Gold Cup. Another of his successes was in the July Stakes of 1796.

Horse racing

But 'Old Dick' who became known as the 'Father of the Turf' has found a lasting niche in horse racing history as the breeder of Diomed, the first winner of the Derby. The race was first held on 4th May 1780 over a distance of one mile. At the time the race was not considered to be of great importance, so few details of it are available. However, the horse's owner was Sir Charles Bunbury, the 'Perpetual President' of the Jockey Club, who had purchased Diomed from Richard Vernon in 1777, and the jockey was Sam Arnull. Diomed was bred at

Newmarket and, at the time of the first Derby, was a high-class three-year-old chestnut.   At that age, the horse won several races having a total value of £5,125 and went on to win many events later.   One of his descendants won the Derby and the Oaks in 1801.

Vernon has another claim to fame, totally unconnected with racing.   He was a keen horticulturalist, and he is believed to have introduced fruit-forcing at Newmarket, where his peaches were well-known.   He is also said to have built a sort of 'extinguisher' at his Church in Newmarket which, if the sermon lasted more than a limited time, descended over the preacher's head and muffled his utterance.

Richard Vernon died at Newmarket on 16th September 1800.

---

3.   THE POOR LAW MAN

THOMAS GILBERT was Member of Parliament for Newcastle-under-Lyme 1763-1768; and Lichfield 1768-1794.

Thomas Gilbert

Thomas Gilbert, the first son of Thomas Gilbert of Cotton, Staffordshire and his wife Elizabeth, was born at Cotton Hall and was baptised at Alton Church on 26th January 1721.   His father was not a rich man, but had a fairly comfortable income of about £300 a year.

Thomas (junior) trained for a legal career, being admitted to the Inner

Temple in 1740, and in 1744 he was called to the Bar. The following year he was commissioned as an ensign into Lord Gower's regiment of foot during the '45 troubles. After the Battle of Culloden he gave the Leveson Gowers legal advice on political affairs and soon afterwards began to devote himself exclusively to that family's affairs. Through Lord Gower's influence Gilbert was appointed in 1753 to a semi-sinecure office - Paymaster of the Charity for the Relief of Widows of Naval Officers - which he held till his death in 1798. In 1758 he became chief agent to the 2nd Earl Gower.

But he was destined for a remarkable political career. It was the 2nd Earl Gower who brought Gilbert into Parliament as M.P. for Newcastle-under-Lyme in 1763. At the next election in 1768 he was made Member for Lichfield and retained that seat till December 1794 when he resigned. Immediately after his election at Newcastle he was given another sinecure - The Comptroller of the Great Wardrobe - which he retained until 1782.

Gilbert's chief memorial in the realm of politics, however, is his legislation concerning the Poor Law, which he began working on soon after entering Parliament. Until this time, each parish was independent as far as Poor Law administration was concerned, and many parishes did not have the resources to cope with the problems of the poor. His first Poor Law Bill, which grouped parishes into unions, passed the Commons in April 1765 but was rejected by the Lords. Further attempts to improve the Poor Law followed, and in 1776 he was responsible for an Act requiring overseers to make returns of sums raised by the poor rates. On 22nd May 1781 Gilbert proposed another bill 'for the better relief and employment of the poor', which was to become the well-known 'Gilbert Act' of 1782. It gave parishes power to combine into unions; encouraged the appointments of both a visitor having executive powers and of a guardian to administer relief; allowed the building of workhouses for the support of children and those unable to work; and sanctioned the provision of outside work to able-bodied males. Sidney and Beatrice Webb said it was 'the most carefully devised, the most elaborate and perhaps the most influential... of Poor Law statutes between 1601 and 1834'. Afterwards Gilbert continued his efforts to reform the Poor Law both in Parliament and with a spate of pamphlets.

But lest it be thought that he was totally immersed in the problems of the poor, he also successfully promoted an Act in 1773 consolidating the law relating to turnpikes, which is regarded as a landmark in the history of English highway administration. On 2nd March 1778, during the War of American Independence, he took the House by surprise in proposing a tax of 25% on government places and pensions, but this failed to become law. Only four years afterwards, however, Thomas Gilbert was asked by the Prime Minister, the Earl of Shelburne, to conduct an inquiry into the value of places and pensions and, as a result, a great number of salaries were diminished and many sinecure places entirely abolished. Gilbert was paid £700 for his labours. But his advocacy of a tax on dogs, his attempt to reform the law concerning vagrants, and legislation for the closing of country alehouses on Sundays (except for travellers) got nowhere. Other ideas from his versatile mind were ahead of his time - doing away with imprisonment for small debts was not adopted until many years later - but his propositions for encouraging the formation of friendly societies by grants from parochial funds were largely provided for in an Act passed in 1793.

Another Act, also known as Gilbert's Act, enabled the Governors of Queen Anne's Bounty to lend capital to promote residences for clergy. In a published tract he made suggestions for the improvement of the police force.

The growing stature of Thomas Gilbert was reflected in the number of the appointments that came his way - he was bencher of the Inner Temple in

1782, reader in 1788 and treasurer 1789. Perhaps the most important occurred on 31st May 1784 when he was made Chairman of the House of Commons Ways and Means Committee, which he held until 1794. The Ways and Means Committee was composed of the whole House of Commons, and sat to consider methods of raising money and supplies.

In addition he was a considerable businessman and in this he cannot be separated easily from his younger brother John. John, who was born at Cotton and was baptised at Alton Church on 4th June 1724, did not have the educational advantages of Thomas, being educated at the village school in Farley. At the age of thirteen he was apprenticed to the firm of Boulton at Birmingham. He grew up there with Matthew Boulton (1728-1809) and they remained life-long friends. In 1742, when his father died and Thomas was studying law in London, John had to return home to look after the estate. He was to become recognised as a remarkable accountant, an outstanding mining engineer, and a gifted canal engineer soon after his appointment as chief agent in 1759 on the Duke of Bridgewater's estate at Worsley, Lancashire. Without doubt he was responsible for a number of major works previously credited to James Brindley (1716-1772).

Thomas Gilbert returned to look after the estate at Cotton in 1757 after completing some work in his capacity of legal agent for the Duke of Bridgewater, and thus John was free to concentrate on his major work of mining and engineering at Worsley. Together, and each in his own sphere, the brothers made a remarkable professional and business pair. Between them they were in coal, lead mining, limestone quarrying, brickmaking, haulage, salt mining, lead pencils and grate polish, farming and land reclamation. It has been said that they, as much as anyone, brought the industrial revolution to their part of North Staffordshire. It is thought that John was the first engineer to employ gunpowder successfully for the mining of salt.

But it was their work relating to the building of canals that played such a vital part in the industrial revolution. The Duke of Bridgewater was the man behind the first major modern canal in this country (appropriately called the Bridgewater) on which work started in 1759. John Gilbert provided the engineering genius and did most of the original survey work both above and below ground. James Brindley did some work at Trentham for Thomas Gilbert in his capacity as land agent to Lord Gower about this time, and Thomas introduced the engineer to the Duke of Bridgewater. Brindley then joined the canal scheme, assisted John Gilbert in surveying, and often had charge of forward operations. The Bridgewater was to be followed by the Trent and Mersey, the Bill being steered through the House of Commons in 1766 by Thomas Gilbert, who may have been the first chairman of the canal company committee. Certainly the brothers held considerable shares in the venture, whilst Josiah Wedgwood, who cut the first sod of the canal at Brownhills, Burslem on 26th July 1766, also invested in the scheme

Site on the Brownhills of the Trent and Mersey Canal

and was treasurer. There was involvement too by the Gilberts in other canals such as the Donnington Wood (with Lord Gower) and the Shropshire.

John Gilbert died on 4th August 1795 at the age of 71. But such was the esteem and friendship held by the Duke of Bridgewater for this retiring and diffident man that he allowed him to be buried in the Egerton family vault at Eccles Church.

John and his wife Lydia, née Bill, whom he had married at Kingsley Church on 3rd January 1744, had a daughter and three sons - Lydia; Thomas, who died before his father; Robert, who became Rector of Settrington, Yorkshire, in the Duke of Bridgewater's gift; and John, who built Clough Hall, Kidsgrove.

After his resignation from Parliament at the end of 1794 Thomas Gilbert retired to his estate at Cotton. But he was not idle, for he built there the Chapel of Ease of St. John the Baptist, which was consecrated on 4th July 1795. His son, also named Thomas, who was baptised on 17th December 1762 at Alton Church, became the first incumbent of the Chapel at Cotton in 1795. His mother, Ann, the daughter of Richard Philips of Hall Green, Checkley, married Thomas Gilbert on 27th January 1762 in Surrey. It is said that Thomas gave her a lottery ticket which drew one of the largest prizes of the year. There was another son of the marriage, Richard, who received a commission in the Navy. Ann died on 22nd April 1770 and was buried at Alton Church on the 30th April. In 1777 Thomas Gilbert married Mary, the daughter of Colonel George Crauford and there was a daughter, Catherine, who was born in 1778 and died 1791.

Thomas Gilbert, who deserves to be better known - as also does his brother - died on 18th December 1798 and is buried beneath the Chapel at Cotton. His wife Mary, who died in 1810, and his daughter lie there too.

---

4.   'LITTLE' MONCKTON

The Hon. Edward Monckton was Member of Parliament for Stafford 1780-1812.

For twenty-six of his thirty-two years as a Member of Parliament for Stafford, Edward Monckton of Somerford served jointly with Richard Brinsley Sheridan. Sheridan often referred to his colleague as 'Little Monckton'.

Monckton was born at Serlby Hall, Nottinghamshire on 3rd November 1744, the fifth son of John Monckton, 1st Viscount Galway, by his second wife Jane, daughter of Henry Westenra of Rathleagh. In 1762 he joined the East India Company's civil service as a writer at Madras, and while in India he made a large fortune. In 1776 he married Sophia, daughter of Lord Pigot of Patshull Hall, and there resulted a large family.

In 1779 he bought the Somerford estate from one of the Barbor family, probably James, and later acquired Brewood Hall, Engleton Hall, and other considerable properties round about. A list of gamekeepers dated 1796 shows manors or lands at Stretton, Brewood, Somerford, Coven, Aspley, Engleton, Water Eaton and Gailey.

In the election of 1774 Stafford returned Hugo Meynell, a Whig, and Richard Whitworth, a Tory, to Parliament. The defeated candidate was Robert Pigot of Patshull, the brother of Lord Pigot and uncle of Monckton's wife. In 1780 Sheridan was anxious to get a seat in Parliament and, having failed to get a nomination to stand for Honiton, his cause was taken up by the Duchess of Devonshire and the Spencer family. It was at Devonshire House that he met Monckton and, as Lord Spencer owned much property in and around Stafford and his influence there was considerable, the town presented itself as a target for Sheridan's political aspirations. With the support and friendship of Monckton, Sheridan was well received in the town, and it seems that Monckton was persuaded to stand in the Whig interest too. Hugo Meynell did not present himself for Stafford again, but Richard Whitworth did. So there was a contest. On the day prior to the election Sheridan entered the town in an open landau, followed by Monckton in an elegant barouche, both vehicles drawn by four horses. The two men were followed by a 'cavalcade of mingled horse and foot, each decorated plenteously with the colours of the candidates'. Flags and banners were flying.

Monckton and Sheridan were duly elected with comfortable majorities, Monckton topping the poll. But it was an expensive business, as all elections were in those days. Even dinners were very costly as the following meal ticket, issued probably for the 1802 elections, shows.

Mr. MONCKTON and Mr. SHERIDAN prefent the Bearer with a DINNER and SIX Quarts of Ale.

No.

E. S.

July 6th.

There is a story in Hackwood's <u>Glimpses of bygone Staffordshire</u> about Monckton's Stafford constituents, who imagined that because they voted for him, they had earned the right to hunt and fish to their heart's content on his properties, of which he was very proud, and which were very well managed. The hunting and fishing were pursued so enthusiastically that Monckton began to fear that none of his game - or even his farm animals and birds - would be left for him to eat! So he was forced to make an agreement with his constituents, under which they could help themselves to his wild game, but must leave him a few of his tame geese, otherwise he would have no Christmas dinner!

In politics Monckton was essentially a Whig, though at certain times, such as that of the French Revolution, he supported the Tories. But his political life was in the sharpest contrast to that of his colleague Sheridan. The latter showed himself to be a great force in Parliament on many important issues of the day, whilst Monckton's 32 years of service are noteworthy because he is thought never to have spoken in Parliament, and rarely voted!

Nevertheless this does not mean that his life was inactive. He enjoyed a large fortune and employed it extensively in the improvement of his estates and for the advantage of the neighbourhood. He was a magistrate for over fifty years.

An officer of the Staffordshire Volunteer Cavalry, 1794

On 4th July 1794 the Staffordshire Volunteer Cavalry (afterwards the Queen's Own Royal Regiment of Staffordshire Yeomanry) was formed with Lord Gower as Colonel. Lt-Col the Hon. Edward Monckton raised the Stafford Troop and remained in command of this unit until 21st March 1800, when Lord Gower retired from his command and Monckton was promoted to Colonel of the Regiment. It was not until 12th December 1829 that he tendered his resignation from the command on account of his age (85) and increasing infirmity.

Monckton died at the 'Old Coaching Inn', Meriden on 1st July 1832 and was interred on 7th July in the family vault in the chancel of Brewood Church.

5.   THE DRAMATIST

RICHARD BRINSLEY SHERIDAN was Member of Parliament for Stafford 1780-1806; Westminster 1806-7; and Ilchester 1807-12.

Richard Brinsley Sheridan

He was born in Dublin on 30th October 1751 to an actor-father, Thomas Sheridan, and writer-mother, Frances Chamberlaine.   He was educated at Harrow 1762-8, and became one of Staffordshire's most distinguished M.Ps.

In 1770 he moved to Bath with his father, his mother now being dead. Elizabeth Linley, a lady friend, the soprano singer ('the Maid of Bath') and daughter of Thomas Linley, a composer, asked Sheridan to escort her to France to escape from Thomas Mathews, a suitor she disliked intensely.   Sheridan was keen to marry the lady himself in spite of objections from both their fathers.   A form of betrothal was entered into while the couple were in France, though Sheridan did not marry Elizabeth until 1773.   The former suitor fought a duel with Sheridan, who won, and he made his opponent publish an apology in a Bath newspaper for the many slanderous statements he had made against him.   That, however, was not the end of the matter, for a second duel fought with swords took place, and this time Sheridan was injured.   The injuries were perhaps not quite as severe as were supposed, since another Stafford M.P., Captain R.H. Gronow, who represented the constituency from 1832-33, comments scathingly in his Reminiscences and recollections that the blood that was supposed to have poured from Sheridan's wounds, 'seems merely to have been the excellent claret of the previous night's debauch'.

Sheridan and his wife settled in London where in 1774 his first play The Rivals was written.   It was produced in the following year at Covent Garden Theatre.   At first it was not a success but gained acclamation after it had been revised.   Shortly afterwards came The Duenna.

On the retirement of the actor David Garrick, Sheridan purchased, with his father-in-law and Dr. James Ford, Garrick's former interest in the Drury Lane Theatre and by mid-1776 Sheridan was Manager. On 8th May 1777 he produced his The School for Scandal there, followed in 1779 by The Critic. In the same year he founded a short-lived paper The Englishman. Soon afterwards he became involved in the agitation for parliamentary reform.

Sheridan had become well-liked by many of the Whig leaders of the day for his great wit and social charm. He joined Charles James Fox, the Liberal leader, in his reforming zeal and this led to a desire on his part to enter Parliament, which he was now able to do because of his ownership of property in the theatre.

He failed in a bid to represent Honiton but was returned for Stafford on 12th September 1780. He probably owed a great deal to the Hon. Edward Monckton for his success. However, bribery at election time was commonplace then and Sheridan had to buy his votes. It has been said that he started the practice of giving £5.5.0 each to most of his supporters to ensure their vote. One of his rivals, Richard Whitworth, tried to have him removed on this account, but he was unsuccessful. Sheridan was re-elected for the 1784-90 Parliament and a statement of his election expenses, drawn up apparently by his agent, is as follows:

	£. s. d.	£. s.
Two hundred and 48 Burgesses paid £5.5s. each		1,302 0
House Rent and Taxes	23 6 6	
Servants	15 12 0	
Ditto, yearly wages	8 8 0	
Coals	10 0 0	
Ale Tickets	40 0 0	
Half the Member's Plate	25 0 0	
Swearing Young Burgesses	10 0 0	
Subscription to the Infirmary	5 5 0	
Ditto, Clergyman's Widows	2 2 0	
Ringers	4 4 0	
One year	£143 17 6	
Multiplied by years 6		863 5
Total Expenses of six years' Parliament, exclusive of expenses incurred during the time of election and your own annual expenses		£2,165 5

The Right Hon. R. B. SHERIDAN,

Presents the Bearer with

Five Shillings and Sixpence

IN ALE.

About this time Stafford society had an elevated distinction in the county and William Horton of Chetwynd House, now the General Post Office, regularly entertained Sheridan and 'all the wits and bright spirits of the age' who accompanied him. William Horton (1750-1832) a wealthy man, apparently had the first boot and shoe factory in Stafford. He supplied his products to places all over England, and had a flourishing export trade to America and the Baltic countries before the Napoleonic Wars. At an election dinner in Stafford Sheridan proposed the toast: 'May the manufacturers of Stafford be trodden under foot by all the world'. It is said that some worthy burgesses were offended by this until it was explained to them!

It was in 1794, at a race-week performance in the Stafford Theatre given by Samuel Stanton's company, that Sheridan first saw the actress Harriot Mellon, who became famous under his management at Drury Lane before marrying firstly the banker Thomas Coutts and then the Duke of St. Albans.

> Mr. SHERIDAN and Mr. MONCKTON prefent the Bearer with a DINNER & SIX Quarts of Ale.
>
> No.   *Paul: Hodgson*   E. S.
>
> July 6th.
>
> DREWRY, PRINTER.

In his Reminiscences and Recollections, Gronow relates a story allegedly illustrating Sheridan's eagerness to please the people of Stafford immediately prior to the 1802 election. Many of those who intended voting for him asked him to find employment for their relatives at the Drury Lane Theatre in return for their favours. One voter had a son looking for employment as an actor; another had a cousin who could paint scenery well; yet another had a nephew who was first-class as a door-keeper; and so on. Sheridan employed them all, and was thus well received when he came on his visits to Stafford before the election. But after the voting was over it was discovered that there was little money at the Theatre to pay all these people, and many received nothing for their labours. Three angry representatives went to Sheridan's London home to protest to him, but his charm overwhelmed them all and he managed to slip away with nothing settled!

But for the 26 years that he represented Stafford (1780-1806) Sheridan certainly proved to be a wonderful orator in Parliament. Paradoxically, his first speech in Parliament was against bribery! He also stood firmly against the American War of Independence. Later he was an Under-Secretary in Rockingham's administration (1782) and a Secretary of the Treasury in the Duke of Portland's Coalition Ministry of 1783. He was also a Privy Councillor for a time, and Treasurer of the Navy 1806-7.

His greatest speech in Parliament, however, was that delivered on the occasion of the impeachment of Warren Hastings. Hastings (1732-1818) was the first Governor-General of British India and had been faced with very difficult courses of action. He made enemies, and was impeached on the grounds of corruption and cruelty in his administration. After a trial lasting from 1788 to

1795 he was unanimously acquitted on every charge. Sheridan's speech on 7th February 1787 moving the third charge against Hastings concerning the Begums of Oude lasted 5 hours and 40 minutes!

Some of Sheridan's speeches in Parliament were against the rigorous imposition of the game laws of the day, which prescribed severe punishments for the poacher caught stealing game. He also came out strongly in favour of the freedom of the press. On the outbreak of the revolution in France, he spoke against any interference by this country in French affairs, though he later became strongly opposed to Napoleon, because of his territorial ambitions.

Although Sheridan had no rivals as a dramatic writer of his day, Drury Lane Theatre did not prosper under him and he became involved in gambling - a curse of life in his times. In 1791 the Drury Lane Theatre was declared unsafe and had to be destroyed. A new building opened three years later was destroyed by fire in 1809.

The financial problems connected with the Theatre prevented his return as M.P. for Stafford in 1812, when it was said that the Stafford voters preferred the money of a leather merchant (Ralph Benson). Since 1806 his lack of finance had compelled him to take whatever seat was offered to him in Parliament, and in the general election of that year he was elected by Westminster. In the following year he was rejected for Westminster but found a seat at Ilchester, which he held until 1812. He did try hard to recapture Stafford in 1812 'but the younger generation of burgesses was as little disposed as the older to vote for any candidate unless he paid each of them the accustomed fee of five guineas'. Sheridan 'would not give them a farthing, and he did not give them money to drink' - an admission of his poor financial state. He still polled 255 votes though.

In 1813 Sheridan, no longer immune as an M.P., was arrested for debt, though his financial affairs were afterwards sorted out. Three years later, on 7th July 1816, he died and was given a magnificent funeral in Westminster Abbey. His wife Elizabeth had died in 1792 and three years afterwards Sheridan married Ester (Hecca) Ogle. He had three daughters, who were all reputed to be very beautiful, and a poet-son, who suffered from ill-health for many years and who died when only 42. Sheridan himself suffered from varicose veins and periodical bouts of depression. He also had difficulties with a throat abcess.

As a politician, Sheridan was a true Whig of the day. It was said of him that 'no more distinguished man ever sat for a Staffordshire constituency, nor in the whole of our history was there a Whig who bestowed greater lustre on the name'. But his plays live on.

6.   THE FOX HUNTING MAN

SIR EDWARD LITTLETON was Member of Parliament for Staffordshire 1784-1812.

Sir Edward Littleton

Like his neighbour, the Hon. Edward Monckton, Sir Edward Littleton seems to have taken very little part in political work, his only recorded speech in Parliament being on 22nd July 1784, against the tax on bricks. It seems too that Sir Edward voted very rarely; his only known recorded vote being in 1788 when he supported Pitt on the illness of King George III.

Sir Edward, the eldest son of Fisher Littleton (1679-1740) of Pipe Ridware, Staffordshire, and his wife Frances, was born on 30th June 1727 and was baptised in Pipe Ridware Church on 28th July of that year. He was educated at Brewood Grammar School and at Emmanuel College, Cambridge, where he was tutored by Richard Hurd, a Classical scholar who was born at Congreve. Hurd was educated at Brewood Grammar School too, and became Bishop of Lichfield (1774-1781) and of Worcester (1781-1808). In 1757, as editor of Horace's works, Hurd dedicated the first volume to Sir Edward, recalling how successfully he applied himself to learning. They kept a close association throughout their lives and in 1799, when they were trustees of Brewood School, provided money to pay for two houses for the extension of the school premises.

In 1742 he succeeded to the estates and baronetcy of his uncle Sir Edward Littleton, 3rd Bart. of Pillaton Hall, an ancient seat in the parish of Penkridge. However, as the Hall occupied a low site and was not in good condition, Sir Edward chose a site for a new seat in Teddesley about three miles away. It is said that the cost of the new Hall was largely defrayed by hoards of coins found in 1742 and 1749 behind panelling at Pillaton Hall. There were twenty-five bags and these realised £15,749. A silver gilt chalice and paten were found too. By 1754 Sir Edward was in occupation at Teddesley Hall, a tall square building built of red brick with stone dressings, having three stories and a basement. The plainness and height of the house, accentuated by falling ground to the south-

Pillaton Hall

west, gave it a rather stark appearance. But the hospitality offered by Sir Edward at Teddesley was generous. William Pitt said, 'His mansion was noted as the scene of old English hospitality, where plenty of roast beef and good ale were provided for all decent visitors, without riot, profusion or wastefulness. The ancient Christmas festivities of Twelfth Night were kept up for the gratification of the inhabitants of the surrounding country as long as the health of the beneficent owner permitted.' The Hall was demolished in 1954.

In 1745 Sir Edward Littleton was commissioned into the regiment of foot raised by Lord Gower (1694-1754, created Viscount Trentham and Earl Gower 1746). As a Captain, Sir Edward commanded a company, which he probably formed when the regiment was raised, and retained his appointment until 1747 when he obtained his release.

On 10th May 1752 Sir Edward married Frances the eldest of the ten children of Christopher Horton of Catton, Staffordshire. She suffered much ill-health and, from the time of her marriage, made numerous visits to Bath, Bristol, Buxton, Scarborough or Harrogate to take the waters or to bathe. She appeared at the assembly rooms of these places and was sometimes accompanied by her husband. But she died childless, aged 49, on 29th August 1781 while on a visit to Tunbridge Wells, and after that Sir Edward seldom travelled other than to London. However, from the time of his marriage it seems that he had considerable influence amongst the Horton family. In 1758 Samuel Hellier, suitor for his sister-in-law, Polly, sought an introduction to the family through him, with subsequent unfortunate results - Hellier was horsewhipped and Sir Edward was fined £100 for assault. Ten years afterwards, on the death of his father-in-law, Littleton became trustee for the six younger children still not provided for.

In local affairs Sir Edward was a very keen supporter of the Staffordshire and Worcestershire Canal. He became a large shareholder in the enterprise, was a member of the management committee when construction began, and gave permission for the Canal to pass for about four miles through his estates, which were very considerable. He inherited the 6,524 acres that had been accumulated around Penkridge by the family since the beginning of the 16th century and consolidated these between 1749 and 1809 by buying out smaller freeholders in Penkridge parish to the tune of 1,911 acres.

He was much concerned with agriculture. He improved the Cannock Heath breed of sheep by crossing with Ross Ryland rams and his experiments were copied by his tenants. He was a great fox-hunting man too and, with his brother-in-law Moreton Walhouse of Hatherton (he married Sir Edward's sister Frances Littleton in 1760), took over the Cannock Wood Hunt in 1774. Sir Edward's mastership ended in 1791 but, although his interest in hunting continued until his death, he did not go out often after 1804.

A fresh fox

Sir Edward died at Teddesley on Sunday 17th May 1812, when the baronetcy expired. His remains, and those of his wife, are in a vault in Penkridge Church. His estates devolved upon his grand-nephew Edward John Walhouse, who assumed the surname and arms of Littleton on 23rd July 1812 and was created Baron Hatherton in 1835.

7. THE ADMIRAL AND HIS BROTHERS

The Hon. JOHN LEVESON GOWER was Member of Parliament for Appleby 1784-90; and Newcastle-under-Lyme 1790-92.

He was born on 11th July 1740, the sixth son of the 1st Earl Gower; his mother, the Earl's third wife, being Mary, the widow of Anthony Grey, Earl of Harold, and the daughter of the 6th Earl of Thanet.

John made the Navy his career. Entering as a boy, he became a Lieutenant on 18th November 1758. He commanded the sloop Kingfisher (14 guns) before being made post captain of the frigate Flamborough (22) on 30th June 1760. Soon afterwards he was captain of the frigate Quebec (32) in the Mediterranean, where (according to Charnock) he carried into Gibraltar a French privateer called Phoenix, carrying 18 guns and one hundred and twenty five men, which he captured off Cape Pelos.

In 1765 he commanded the ship of the line Africa (64) on the coast of Guinea and in the West Indies; the frigate Aeolus (32) in the Mediterranean in 1766-7; the frigate Pearl (32) from 1769 to 1772 at home and Newfoundland; and the guardship Albion (74) at Plymouth in 1774. In 1774 he was captain of the ship Valiant (74) in the Channel.

On 6th July 1773 John married Frances, daughter of Admiral Edward Boscawen. A son, John, was born on 25th June 1774.

The Hon. John Leveson Gower was closely connected with Admiral Augustus Keppel and Admiral Sir Charles Saunders with whom he became a close friend and a trusted follower. Leveson (as he was always called) served under Keppel in the indecisive action off Ushant on 27th July 1778 whilst in Valiant, which lost five men killed and twenty six wounded. John Jervis of Meaford, Stone, later to become Earl of St. Vincent, also served at Ushant as Captain of the captured French ship Foudroyant (80). When controversy broke out later in the year between Keppel and his second-in-command Sir Hugh Palliser over the conduct of this action, Leveson Gower kept himself out of the dispute, but when Palliser demanded that Keppel be court-martialled and this was agreed to, Leveson Gower, with the majority of the captains who had taken part off Ushant, spoke up for Keppel who was unanimously and honourably acquitted. In a subsequent court-martial Palliser was also acquitted, but criticised. Shortly afterwards Leveson Gower signed a memorial to King George III praying for Palliser's dismissal, and resigned his ship. He did not serve again until April 1782 when Lord Howe (1726-99) was appointed Commander-in-Chief of the Channel Fleet and hoisted his flag as Admiral of the Blue in the 1st rate ship of the line Victory (110) (Captain Henry Duncan) at Spithead with Leveson Gower as his Captain of the

H.M. ships *Agamemnon, Captain, Vanguard, Elephant* and *Victory*

Fleet, a temporary admiralty appointment entitling the holder to be considered as a flag officer and to share in prize money accordingly. His special duty would be to keep up the discipline of the fleet. Leveson served in this capacity in the Channel and at the relief of Gibraltar, where he was mentioned in the despatches of Lord Howe. When peace came Leveson Gower quitted his command.

In January 1783, though not in Parliament and not yet of flag rank, he was appointed by Lord Howe, who was now First Lord of the Admiralty, as a junior Lord at the Admiralty, a seat which he kept, apart from one short break, until 1790.

On 17th June 1785 a full board of the Admiralty approved the promotion of Prince William (later King William IV) to the rank of lieutenant. He had not received any special favour for, although he had spent two years on shore, he had been a midshipman since 1779 and this would have been thought excessive by most of the well-connected. Immediately he repaired to Portsmouth to join his ship, Hebe (44), a frigate originally captured from the French, commanded by Captain Edward Thornbrough (later Admiral Sir Edward Thornbrough). Leveson Gower hoisted a broad penant as Commodore in this ship for a cruise with his squadron round Great Britain, and Prince William, in a letter to his father (King George III) sent from Hebe in Carrickfergus Bay on 4th August 1785, said '... we have begun to know our Commodore better: he is a most attentive and rigid officer, but unfortunately is passionate at times: however it is immediately over.'

Two years afterwards Commodore Leveson Gower was in Edgar (74) with Captain Charles Thompson in command of the Channel Squadron (six ships of the line and several frigates) and, on 24th September 1787, became Rear-Admiral of the Blue, the lowest position in the then hierarchy of admirals. In March 1788 Prince William was appointed captain of the frigate Andromeda (32) and for a short period his ship was one of Leveson Gower's squadron, which comprised six ships of the line and two frigates.

It was during the time of his service (1784) at the Admiralty that he was elected as Member of Parliament for Appleby in Westmorland. Four speeches by him are recorded between 1784 and 1790, all on Admiralty business. In 1790 he was elected M.P. for Newcastle-under-Lyme. However, his political career was comparatively undistinguished as his heart lay in the Navy.

In the summer of 1790, during the period of tension between Spain and Britain over the ownership of Nootka Sound, Vancouver Island and the seizure by the Spanish of English ships there, a mobilization of the English fleet took place. Admiral Lord Howe, who had Leveson Gower as Rear Admiral, commanded the fleet of 35 sail of the line. Prince William, now Duke of Clarence, was in Leveson Gower's squadron as captain of Valiant (74) and, in a letter to his brother the Prince of Wales (later George IV), he mentions that 'Admiral Leveson Gower is a truly respectable character'. Howe cruised for several weeks between Ushant and Scilly, exercising continually in tactics and in a new code of signals upon which he had been working. Confronted by this display of strength, Spain abated her demands over the Sound and a peaceful settlement followed. The fleet returned to Spithead in mid September 1790 when most of the ships paid off. On 21st September Leveson Gower became Rear Admiral of the White.

Neptune

Whilst shaving at his house at Bill Hill, near Wokingham, John Leveson Gower had an apoplectic fit and died on 15th August 1792.

There was a poll in September 1792 to fill the seat at Newcastle-under-Lyme. However, for some time many people in this town had not been happy with the influence the Leveson Gowers of Trentham had exercised over the elections. This influence was exerted by their control of the admission to the register of those entitled to vote; by lavish hospitality at their home at Trentham; and by leasing houses to many of the voters at very low rents. Such measures were not, of course, by any means uncommon in those days.

Gradually, opposition to the Leveson Gowers became more open. One broadsheet, distributed at the time of the 1790 poll, when John Leveson Gower was elected, contained a parody on a biblical passage and referred scathingly to the Leveson Gowers as the chosen of the Lord. The Leveson Gowers fought back by creating freemen of Newcastle specially for election purposes, but gradually their influence in Newcastle politics declined and eventually disappeared. Even in the 1792 poll, although a Gower Whig (William Egerton) stood, Thomas Fletcher (1737-1802) who had contested the seat in 1790 beat him by two votes. However, Thomas Fletcher, whose family represented the constant opposition to the Gower interest, lost the seat on scrutiny and Egerton was declared elected - a close call for the Gower Whigs on this occasion.

Two of John's half-brothers, their mother being Lady Evelyn Pierrepont, were Staffordshire M.Ps. too. The more important, perhaps politically the most important of all the Leveson Gowers, was GRANVILLE (1721-1803) who entered Parliament for Bishop's Castle in 1744 but was returned for Westminster from 1747 to 1754. On 15th April 1754 he was elected M.P. for Lichfield but served only until 25th December of that year as he became the 2nd Earl Gower on the death of his father. From this time he held high court and political offices almost continuously - Lord of the Admiralty; Lord Privy Seal; Master of the Horse; Master of the Wardrobe; Lord Chamberlain; Lord President of the Council; Lord Privy Seal. He was made a Knight of the Garter in 1771 and created Marquess of Stafford on 1st March 1786. He was Lord Lieutenant of Staffordshire from 1755-1800, High Steward of Stafford in 1769, and died at Trentham Hall on 26th October 1803. It is said that he refused the office of Prime Minister after the fall of Lord Shelburne's ministry in March 1783.

The Hon. RICHARD LEVESON GOWER (1726-1753), the 4th son of the 1st Earl Gower, was elected M.P. for Lichfield in 1747 and served in this capacity until his death on 19th October 1753. He was an Under-Secretary of State to the Duke of Bedford from 1749 to 1751, was a very good cricketer, and spent much of his time at White's Club, which he joined in 1747.

8.   THE INDUSTRIALIST

SIR ROBERT PEEL was Member of Parliament for Tamworth 1790-1820.

Sir Robert Peel, 1750 – 1830

The third son of Robert 'Parsley' Peel and his wife Elizabeth née Howarth, he is said to have been born in the family farm house, 'Peel Fold', near Oswald-twistle, Lancashire, in April 1750, but there is a strong body of opinion which declares that he was born in a farm house in Fish Lane, Blackburn. However, he was certainly baptised in Blackburn Parish Church on 23rd April 1750.

'Parsley' Peel (the nickname came from his parsley-leaf design on one of his cotton prints) was a partner in the very successful firm of Howarth (his brother-in-law), Peel and Yates of Church, near Blackburn; a firm that could claim the honour of being founders of the great Lancashire calico-printing industry. After some years the partners disbanded, Howarth and Yates moving to Bury, whilst Peel stayed at Church. 'Parsley' Peel possessed much inventive and mechanical skill and, with James Hargreaves (1720-1778) of 'spinning jenny' fame, made great improvements to a new form of carding cylinder for use in the Blackburn cotton mills.   In 1779 there was rioting against the new spinning-jennies and 'Parsley' decided to move southward to a more peaceable area.   He chose Burton-upon-Trent. Cotton spinning had never been a major industry of Staffordshire, but Peel soon became an important figure in the town.   On his retirement about 1792 he returned to Lancashire where he died at Ardwick in 1795, but some of his younger sons carried on the business at Burton.

Robert, 'Parsley' Peel's third son, was educated at Blackburn Grammar School, but learned the trade of calico printing from his father.   He grew up in the firm belief that he had it within his power to succeed by hard work, and therefore spent much of his time in studying commerce and manufacturing.

In 1773 he became a partner in the firm of Jonathan Howarth (his uncle) and William Yates at Bury. The mills were very busy and produced great wealth. Robert, in spite of his love for business, had qualities of an originator and a reformer. He began the practice of bringing pauper children from the London workhouses to serve in the mills, but they were fed, clothed and housed adequately. Sometimes, however, Peel's instructions were ignored by overseers and as a result his mills were for some time as bad as any as regards working conditions. Indeed one of them was involved in a fever epidemic in 1784 which provoked a public enquiry into factory conditions.

On 8th July 1783 Robert Peel married Ellen Yates (1766-1803), the daughter of one of his partners and they moved into a new home, Chamber Hall, in Bury. By this time Peel was already a wealthy man and virtual head of a flourishing concern, for his partner Howarth had retired and Yates increasingly left matters to Peel. He had worked very hard and was in the forefront in the use of new inventions that would save labour costs.

Robert and Ellen had a large family, and most of their eleven children were born at Chamber Hall. The first entry concerning the family in the parish register of St. Peter's Church, Drayton Bassett, concerns the burial of their child Anne in August 1799. Ten years earlier Peel, perhaps stimulated by the family's success in Burton, decided to start a cotton industry in Tamworth and make his home there. The transition, however, took some time. Castle Mill was leased for his cotton enterprises; the banqueting hall in the Castle was used as a forge in connexion with a factory that he erected in Lady Meadow; mills for cotton spinning and calico printing were started at Fazeley and Bonehill. In 1790 he acquired land at Drayton and elsewhere, lands and property in Tamworth itself, including 120 houses, and finally in 1796 he completed the purchase of Drayton Manor. By the end of the century a new Hall had been built but it

Drayton Manor

is probable that from the start Robert Peel desired a permanent position in the county, and his purchases in Tamworth left the way clear to succeed to one of the parliamentary seats previously held by the Thynnes, the family name of the Marquis of Bath from whom Peel had acquired much of his property. Robert Peel became M.P. for Tamworth in 1790. He was to hold the seat as a Tory through seven successive parliaments covering 30 years.

In Parliament he was a keen supporter of Pitt and, although his sympathies when the French Revolution began were with the Revolution, he changed his position when it grew violent in character. In 1797 when 'persons of affluent fortunes' were allowed to make voluntary contributions to Pitt's war budget, the firm of Yates and Peel put themselves down for £10,000 - a huge sum. Peel assisted in the formation of the Lancashire Fencibles and the Tamworth Armed Association and, in 1798, he raised and commanded six companies of the Bury Loyal Volunteers - mainly from his employees. The following year he was made a baronet. In 1799 he had spoken strongly for union with Ireland and his speech was printed in Dublin.

He was a wealthy man but he was generous and, in his later career, was associated with many benevolent bodies; for example he became vice-president of the Society for Benefiting the Condition of the Poor and in 1801 contributed £1,000 to its funds. In 1802 he carried through Parliament the Health and Morals of Apprentices Act, which limited the hours of work to twelve, forbade night employment and made provision for clothing, education and conditions of work. He also acted as parliamentary spokesman for Robert Owen and other reformers, resulting in an Act of 1819 to help cotton-mill children. In Tamworth he founded Sir Robert Peel's School which he endowed with £6,000 in 1820, and he was High Steward of the town from 1811 until his death at Drayton Manor on 3rd May 1830. The verdict of history is that he was one of the pioneers of the greatness of modern England. Certainly he was a decisive figure in the Peel family; from working with his own hands in the mills he became an M.P., a baronet and a wealthy landowner.

His wife Ellen had died at Buxton on 28th December 1803 and was buried at Drayton on 3rd January 1804. On 18th October 1805, Sir Robert married Susanna Clerke who was then aged fifty-two. Ellen did not live long enough to see her first two sons Robert and William Yates Peel (1789-1858) enter Parliament; Robert became M.P. for Cashel, Ireland in 1809, whilst William Yates Peel followed his father to represent Tamworth in 1820. When Robert was born on 5th February 1788 it is said that his father thanked God on his knees and pledged his son to the service of his country. Young Robert obtained a parliamentary seat as soon as he came of age and sat in the House of Commons for the rest of his life. His first ministerial appointment came when he was twenty-two; he was Home Secretary at thirty-four and Prime Minister at forty-six. The pledge was fulfilled.

Sculpture in St. Stephen's Chapel

LORD GRANVILLE LEVESON GOWER (later Earl Granville) was Member of Parliament for Lichfield 1795-99; and Staffordshire 1799-1815.

1st Earl Granville

When Thomas Gilbert resigned his seat in Parliament at the end of 1794, the Gower interest had a ready replacement for the City of Lichfield in Lord Granville Leveson Gower. He was returned unopposed on 14th January 1795, although he was only just of age. He was born at Trentham on 12th October 1773; the third and youngest son of Granville, 1st Marquess of Stafford by his third wife Lady Susannah Stewart.

Lord Granville Leveson Gower was educated at Dr Kyle's school at Hammersmith, then at Donnington, Shropshire, under the Rector, the Rev. John Chappel Woodhouse, who became Dean of Lichfield Cathedral in 1807. Leveson Gower matriculated at Christ Church, Oxford on 29th April 1789. Ten years later he became a Doctor of Civil Law.

After one or two excursions into the field of diplomacy in 1797 and 1798, he was appointed by William Pitt (1759-1806) the Prime Minister and great friend of the Marquess of Stafford as a Lord of the Treasury in 1800 in the room of the Hon. J.T. Townshend.

On 19th July 1804 he became a Privy Councillor and later that year was Ambassador to St. Petersburg when England was forming the third coalition against Napoleon. His mission was to persuade the Emperor Alexander to join the coalition and, although he did conclude a treaty, it proved inoperable. He returned to England in 1805. However, he was appointed to a second term at St. Petersburg in April 1807 though he did not arrive there until the end of June, and his stay lasted only until November when Russia, then being completely under Bonaparte's influence, formally broke off diplomatic relations. England and Russia were then virtually in a state of war.

On 1st July 1809 Lord Granville Leveson Gower became a member of the Cabinet as Secretary for War but he resigned in October of that year when Spencer Perceval succeeded the Duke of Portland as Prime Minister. Perceval was assassinated in the lobby of the House of Commons on 11th May 1812 by

John Bellingham, who felt he was forced to take justice into his own hands to remedy a grievance that originated in a visit he made to Archangel and in which Leveson Gower, as Ambassador, was involved. Bellingham felt that the British representatives in Russia should have come to his aid, and said at his trial '... it would have been more fortunate for Mr Perceval, had Lord Gower received the ball which terminated the life of the latter gentleman'.

Leveson Gower's seat in Parliament became vacant when he took the Chiltern Hundreds on 31st July 1815, and on 12th August he was created Viscount Granville of Stone Park. He resided mainly in England for the next eight years, taking occasional part in the debates of the House of Lords. It was in one of these, on 24th April 1823, concerning Lord Ellenborough's motion for an address of censure on George Canning (1770-1827) the Foreign Secretary, that Viscount Granville carried an amendment in favour of Canning, with whom he had a close personal friendship. The following November Granville was appointed Ambassador to the Hague. His residence there was short as, in the autumn of 1824 Canning made him Ambassador to Paris. On 9th June 1825 he was invested with the Grand Cross of Bath, in accordance with the custom of the time, by the King of France at the Tuileries. In this office, as in all others, Lord Granville proved very reliable and trustworthy, though he was sometimes criticised for his slowness in submitting his despatches. In 1828 he was recalled but when Earl Grey became Prime Minister in 1830, Granville was reappointed Ambassador to Paris and he stayed in this post, with only one short break, until 1841 when he retired.

At the time of the Reform Bill of 1832 he was so strongly in support of the Whig position for correcting many of the electoral abuses that he came specially from Paris to vote in its favour. On 10th May 1833 his services to the country were recognised by his being created Baron Leveson of Stone and Earl Granville.

In 1840 a slight touch of paralysis gave warning that the end of his long diplomatic career was near and he died, after a long illness, on 8th January 1846. He was buried at Stone.

He married Henrietta Elizabeth Cavendish, daughter of the 5th Duke of Devonshire, on 24th December 1809 and there were three sons and two daughters of the union.

Like many men of this period, Lord Granville was an inveterate gambler and he had been known to lose a fortune in an evening's play. He was reckoned to be the best whist player of his day and the gambling fraternity in Paris knew him as 'le Wellington des jouers'.

REFERENCES

Works used in more than one Chapter

Burke's Peerage

Cockayne's complete Peerage

Dictionary of National Biography

Report from the Select Committee on Stafford Borough. 1834

Staffordshire Advertiser

Victoria History of the County of Stafford (several volumes)

Butters, P.   Stafford. 1979

Namier, Sir L. and Brooke, J.   The House of Commons, 1754-1790. 1964

Simms, R.   Bibliotheca Staffordiensis. 1894

Staffordshire Parish Register Society's printed parish registers (several volumes)

Wedgwood, J.C.   Staffordshire Members of Parliament, Parts II and III. 1920/22 and 1933

Specific books numbered as per Chapters

1. Chetwynd-Stapylton, H.E.   The Chetwynds of Ingestre. 1892

1. Sedgwick, R.   The House of Commons, 1715-1754. 1970

2. Mortimer, R.   The Jockey Club. 1958

3. Lead, P.   The Trent and Mersey Canal. 1979

3. Lindsay, J.   The Trent and Mersey Canal. 1979

3. Malet, H.   The canal duke. 1961

3. Robey, J.A. and Porter, L. The copper and lead mines of Ecton Hill, Staffordshire. 1961

4. An Octogenarian   Sheridan and his times. 1859

4. Webster, P.C.G.   The records of the Queen's Own Royal Regiment of Staffordshire Yeomanry. 1870

5. An Octogenarian   Sheridan and his times. 1859

5. Cherry, J.L.   Stafford in olden times. 1890

5. Gronow, R.H.   Reminiscences and recollections. 1964 abr.ed.

5. Rae, W.F.   Sheridan. 1896

6. Farr, M.W.   Sir Edward Littleton's fox-hunting diary, 1774-89 (In: Collections for a history of Staffordshire. 1970)

6. Pitt, W.   A topographical history of Staffordshire.   1817

6. Tildesley, J.C.   A history of Penkridge. 1886

7. Aspinall, A.   The later correspondence of George III, Vol. I. 1962

7. Aspinall, A.   The correspondence of George, Prince of Wales, 1770-1812, Vols, I and III. 1963-4

7. Charnock, J.   Biographia navalis, Vol. IV. 1798

8. Gash, N.   Mr. Secretary Peel. 1961

8. Smith, C.   Drayton Manor. 1978

9. Fitzmaurice, Lord E. The life of Granville George Leveson Gower, second Earl Granville. 1906

9. Gillen, M.   Assassination of the Prime Minister. 1972

Documents and Theses

Parish registers in the County Record Office (several)

Hawkes, R.A.   Corruption in Newcastle-under-Lyme. 1975 (thesis)

3. Lead, P.   Thomas and John Gilbert. 1982 (thesis)

6. Item 523 in William Salt Library

6. Item D1413/2 in County Record Office

Hilton Hall